Interview with
Cleopatra
& Other Famous Rulers

Published in 2022 by Welbeck Children's Books Limited
An imprint of the Welbeck Publishing Group
Based in London and Sydney.
www.welbeckpublishing.com

Designer: RockJaw Creative
Design Manager: Matt Drew
Senior Editor: Jenni Lazell
Production: Melanie Robertson

ISBN: 978-1-78312-853-2

Printed in the UK

10 9 8 7 6 5 4 3 2 1

Interview with
Cleopatra

& Other Famous Rulers

Written by
**Andy
Seed**

Illustrated by
**Gareth
Conway**

WELBECK

Contents

Introduction

Have you ever wanted to be the BOSS? The big cheese? The leader? What's it like being the head honcho who shouts out orders all day and gets to make the big decisions? Well, I have never been in charge (some would say for obvious reasons), but I wanted to know, so I set out on a MISSION.

Of course, I could have found out by asking some of today's leaders. Maybe had a prattle with a president or a chat with a chancellor. But I decided it would be FAR more interesting to talk to some emperors or queens or sultans—you know, the kind who sit on big thrones in castles and perhaps walk around with an enormous sword.

There is just one teeny problem. THEY'RE ALL DEAD. It's very inconsiderate of them, I know, and they could have made it easier for me to interview them, I'm sure, but I wasn't going to let a small thing like

DEATH get in the way of a good gabfest with some of history's greatest rulers.

I set to work to solve the problem, and I had a GINORMOUS stroke of luck. Some of you (the good ones) may have read my other Q&A book series, beginning with *Interview with a Tiger and Other Clawed Beasts Too*. Well, to enable me talk to sharks, polar bears, and giant squid, I managed to invent a marvelous machine, the TRANIMALATOR. I wondered if, with a few adjustments, this could be adapted into a TIME MACHINE . . .

So I swapped the device's waffle maker for a chin rest—and what do you know? It didn't work. Hitting it with a large hammer was oddly unsuccessful too. So I did some serious research and watched nine sci-fi movies from the 1960s. Most other time-travelers it seems have some kind of alien help or the handy intervention of a mysterious asteroid. Difficult. I called a friend at NASA, and she suggested firing some dark matter into a black hole during a solar storm to enable stellar flux reversal. I got my friend Baz to help—and it worked!

With my time-traveling tranimalator fully functional, I've been able to zip back into the past and talk to some of history's biggest, baddest, brainiest bosses. I discovered that rulers back then could mostly just DO WHAT THEY LIKED. Some of them were really scary, others cunning and ruthlessly smart, but all were powerful. I saw riches that made me gawp, vast palaces, and the rewards of plundering from conquered lands or smart trading.

I visited kings and rulers all around the world, from various periods and many cultures. Wow, they were SO DIFFERENT. But all had one thing in common: a ripping story to tell. I heard from their own lips how they came to power, the troubles they faced, and what their dreams and fears were. I was amazed at what they told me, and I think you will be too.

Andy Seed

~ An interview with ~
Cleopatra

For this interview, I travel back to the year 32 BCE, to ancient Egypt, to meet possibly the most famous queen that ever lived . . .

Q. Hello, uh, Your Majesty, it's very good of you to meet me. This is exciting—I've never chatted to a pharaoh before.

A. I have met many strange people in my time but nothing as strange as you.

Q. That's because I am from the future!

A. So my advisers tell me . . . quite a claim. Well, we rulers are always eager to discover what tomorrow brings.

Q. Ah, you want to know the weather forecast? Hang on while I just open the app . . .

A. What is that curious object? Some kind of divining stone? An amulet?

Q. No, just my old smartphone.
A. A what?

Q. Uh, it's a device for, well, ooh, this is going to be quite tricky to explain . . . Oh, no WiFi. Well, I suppose it is 32 BCE and we are in the desert . . .
A. Stranger, what exactly do you want?

Q. May I just ask you a few questions? It won't take long.
A. Hmmm, very well. But if I think you're a Roman spy I will have my soldiers cut you into dog food.

Q. Fair enough, gulp. So, uh, what was your childhood like?
A. I was born and raised here in the Royal Palace in Alexandria. My father was Ptolemy XII, Pharaoh, so my childhood was not exactly ordinary.

Q. It's a very grand building—lots of bling.
A. Of course, it must be suitable for rulers of the mighty kingdom of Egypt. And now it is mine.

Q. Uh, is that Greek you're speaking, not Egyptian?
A. Correct. I speak many languages, being highly educated. We rulers use Greek because the powerful

warrior Alexander the Great invaded this land 300 years ago. He brought Greek culture here, and this city is named after him. Of course, I speak Egyptian too, which is one of the reasons I'm popular—my father never bothered to learn it. Which land are you from, anyway?

Q. I'm from Britain. It's a big island far to the north—think Stonehenge, not pyramids. Or maybe shopping centers these days.

A. Ah, Britannia? Julius Caesar invaded it in 55 BCE, I recall. He said it was cold and damp and the people were wild, unruly mobs with painted skin.

Q. Yep, that's the place. Still the same today. So do you rule Egypt on your own?

A. Pah! There's a foolish law that I must govern with a male. In theory my son Caesarion rules with me, but he is just a little boy. Before that I had to put up with sharing power with my useless brothers.

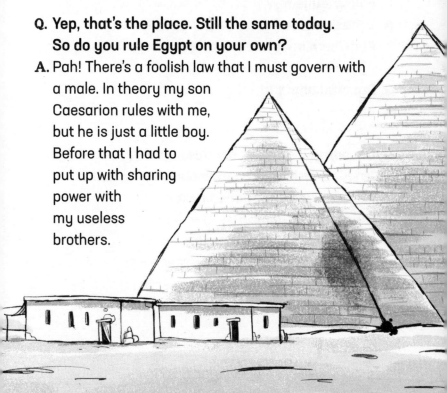

Q. Oh, I see. So where are they now?

A. Tragically they are no longer with us. They both met, um, an unfortunate end . . .

Q. Oh dear, what happened?

A. It all began when my father the pharaoh died in 51 BCE. I was the eldest, and smartest, so should have ruled as queen alone, but because of tradition, my younger brother Ptolemy was made co-ruler with me, ugh.

Q. Yeah, it's bad enough sharing candy with your kid bro . . . but wait, I thought your dad was called Ptolemy?

A. My father was Ptolemy XII, my brother was Ptolemy XIII. It's another tiresome tradition.

Q. Ptolemy about it!

A. What?

Q. Oh, sorry, it's a pun—because we don't say the "p" . . . considered hilarious in later Britannia. Anyway, what happened next?

A. I had to marry him.

Q. YOUR BROTHER?

A. And he was only 10.

Q. WHATTTT! That is A SHOCKER!

A. It wasn't a real marriage. More like an old Egyptian custom.

Q. It's still weird. Anyway, how did your mini hubby-king-brother croak?

A. The fool wanted to rule alone when he was 13. Pressured by his greedy advisers, he tried to grab power and get the army on his side. I had to flee for my life.

Q. That's teenagers for you . . .

A. It was an outrage! I was a successful queen too, helping the country become safer and richer. I had built supplies of food to guard against times of flood and drought, and I dealt with the lawless gangs of robbers that plagued the people. But Ptolemy did not last long—Rome came to my rescue. Well, Julius Caesar.

Q. The Roman guy! Sorry. Carry on, Cleo.

A. Hmmmm. Anyway, Rome is a mighty state that rules many of the lands around the Mediterranean Sea. And just like here, there are always rival leaders trying to gain power. Sixteen years ago it was Caesar and Pompey, two strong Roman generals with soldiers behind them. Julius was gaining the upper hand, so Pompey came here to Egypt, thinking he would be safe.

Q. But he wasn't?

A. Exactly. My reckless little brother saw a chance to get Caesar on his side, to help get rid of me. He sent his men to kill Pompey and cut off his head.

Q. Yikes! What then?

A. Caesar came here to Alexandria. He wanted to sort out the mess in Egypt and gain some of our famed wealth. I saw my chance to meet him and get him on my side. Of course, my brother was still in charge in the city at that point, so I had to be sneaky and clever. I got some trusted friends to hide me in a rolled-up rug and smuggle it into the palace so I could meet Caesar.

Q. What did he say?

A. Plenty. I was just 21 but full of passion and ability to lead. He was impressed that I could speak Latin as

well as Greek, Egyptian, and more. He soon realized I was a far better ruler than that squirt Ptolemy. So, yes, I charmed him, won him over, and he agreed to help me get rid of my upstart rival.

Q. Did Ptolemy fight?

A. He tried to get his feeble army to take us on, but he was no match for my forces plus Caesar's Roman ships at the Battle of the Nile. He drowned trying to swim away in his armor . . .

Q. Gosh. So did Julius Caesar stay with you after that?

A. Good question. We were a couple for a while, and even had a baby together, but he had a wife back in Rome and had to return eventually. I went there too, which was stupendously awkward . . .

Anyway, to make things worse, many important Romans thought Caesar was getting too powerful. A group of them hatched a plot and stabbed him to death in 44 BCE.

Q. Eek, how do you handle all the DANGER in these times?

A. A person in my position cannot escape it. Anyway, I returned to Egypt for safety, and things were quieter for a while until the next Roman general arrived.

Q. Who was that?

A. Mark Anthony. He had been a close friend of Caesar's. He came to see me and we were, uh, drawn together. Having the protection of a powerful Roman leader makes me more secure here as queen, so it was a smart move, and I liked him. Although I did have to deal with a second brother.

Q. Another Ptolemy?

A. Yes, he had a little accident with some poison, poor boy. But Mark Anthony is still here, and we are together with our three children. Egypt is now peaceful and prosperous.

Q. No trouble now?

A. Oh there's always trouble. Anthony has a rival in Rome named Octavian. It's the usual story—he wants to grab power. He's not very happy with us and has plans to come over to fight us, but we can deal with him. Wait, you're from the future—you must know what happens! Do we win?

Q. Um, I don't know, I missed that history lesson in school. I was away with a sprained chin.

A. Why don't you ask your Phartsmone thing?

Q. My smartphone? No signal, whew . . .

A. Are you HIDING SOMETHING from me? Maybe you are one of Octavian's spies! GUARDS!

Yikes! Come on tranimalator—take me back to drizzling Britannia, NOW!

The end of Cleopatra

What happened next?

- The Roman general Octavian defeated Cleopatra and Mark Anthony in a battle.
- They escaped to Egypt separately, with Octavian's soldiers in pursuit.
- Many people believe that Mark Anthony killed himself because he thought Cleopatra was dead. Whoops, she wasn't . . .
- The story goes that she then poisoned herself (some say from a snake bite, ouch) and died, in 30 BCE.
- Octavian was later known as Augustus, and he became the very first Roman emperor.

Was Cleopatra beautiful?

We don't know what she looked like for sure, but she certainly wore eye-popping clothes. There are some ancient images found on these things:

- Coins
- Wall paintings
- Sculptures
- Vases

In some of these she looks noble and powerful rather than beautiful. Roman historians say she was smart, brave, and charming. It's clear she was in many ways **AMAZING**.

Why is Cleo so famous?

- There were not many female rulers in the ancient world.
- She was the last pharaoh.
- She caused a scandal in Rome by having affairs with two married men.
- Her story has been told by great writers such as William Shakespeare.
- There are OODLES of books and movies about her!

CleoFACTra

1. She became queen when she was just a **teenager.**
2. Cleo was the **richest** woman in the world.
3. She had an extra-fancy royal boat covered in **gold.**
4. She sometimes dressed like Isis, a **winged goddess.**

ITALY

ROME

GREECE

ALEXANDRIA

EGYPT

An interview with
Alexander the Great

We're now way back in the year 323 BCE in the ancient city of Babylon to have a chat with one of history's most successful and feared commanders.

Q. Is it OK to call you Alex?
A. Be gone, tiresome buffoon. I don't want any more feeble entertainers.

Q. Sorry, uh, Your Greatness. These are my normal clothes. I'm not here to perform. I'm from a far distant land, hoping to find some answers.
A. What land? I've never seen you before. How did you get past my guards? Ah, perhaps you stole into the palace to prove your courage and cunning? Bravo!

You must be a strong leader, perhaps a worthy ally . . . How many men do you have at your command? Calvary? Or do you favor archers? Where is your fortress?

Q. Wow, I thought I was asking the questions! Um, I'm not really the ninja type—more of, well, a *scribe* from, um, a faraway kingdom. Does that make sense?

A. Who is the ruler of your kingdom?

Q. We have a queen: Elizabeth.

A. Unusual. Does she wear armor and ride into battle?

Q. Not often—she's in her 90s.

A. You are wasting my time! Do you know who I am? Alexander III of Macedonia. King, general, explorer, scholar, and ruler of the largest empire the world has ever known! Now go!

Q. All right, sorry, Your Royal Hugeness. Shall I take my time machine to Persia and interview King Darius instead?

A. Darius? But he's dead. A time machine? It is not possible . . . and yet some instinct tells me to believe you. What do you want to know?

Q. You became a king at age 20. How did that happen?

A. It was always fated. My father was Philip of Macedonia, warrior king of northern Greece. He was a powerful man who won countless victories, but this brought him many enemies. One of them stabbed him at my sister's wedding and he died. I took the throne—I was ready, even as a young man.

Q. How?

A. Princes like me were trained to lead from birth. As a boy, I was taught to read and play music but also to ride, to fight, to hunt. I wanted to be the best at all things. My father had me tutored by Aristotle, one of the wisest men alive. My mother, Olympias, made sure I was first among rivals to succeed to the throne. I had to be strong, ruthless.

Q. Yeah, who needs ruth! Anyway, is the story about you taming a rowdy horse true?

A. Ah, Bucephalus, my mighty steed! Yes, at age twelve or so I bet my father I could ride him. No one else could, but I saw he was afraid of his own shadow. I calmed him and made him mine. Old Ox-head! That divine animal carried me into battle for decades, across ten thousand miles. I miss him so much.

Q. So you were king of Macedonia in Greece, but what made you want to go and conquer the world?

A. What indeed? Do you know what GLORY is? I know better than any man . . . I was a winner, but I didn't want to just win at games or horse races or even fights—I wanted to win battles, take lands, create a glorious and vast empire such as the world had never known. And I did! It was always inside me, this burning ambition, but Aristotle truly lit the flame when he gave me a copy of *The Iliad* and I read about the mythical warrior-god Achilles and his great deeds. I wanted to be him: UNSTOPPABLE.

Q. Wow, I certainly wouldn't have tried to stop you! So why did you go and conquer Persia first?

A. The Greeks had always had trouble from the Persians, that great empire to the east. I also admired them in many ways. I read much about their first great king, Darius. His accomplishments were magnificent. But back then in 334 BCE their leader was Darius III, a lesser man and our enemy. I had to deal with him.

Q. So what was your plan?

A. I was already leading soldiers when I was 17 and 18. I noticed the different strategies of the commanders—what worked and why, and what failed. But the most obvious step was to have the largest army possible, so as a young king I brought the many city-states of Greece together so we were united against the Persians.

Q. Please explain.

A. You really are from another time! Greece has long been divided into small territories. Some, like Athens and Thebes, were only a single city with the land around them, with their own leaders. Each only had a small, weak military force. I convinced them that we needed to join together to be strong and defeat the Persians, who might have invaded us at any time.

Q. With you as the leader by any chance?

A. Of course! Macedonia was powerful, and the other city-states saw my skill as a leader in dealing with my father's enemies after he was killed. I created an army of 50,000 men. We marched into Asia and nothing could resist us! We went into North Africa and took control of Egypt, and then we headed east again and fought Darius. I beat him twice. Persia was mine.

Q. Ah yes, was it Cleopatra who told me that her city was named after you?

A. Cleo who? Anyway, we raided the Persian capital, Persepolis, and carted away mountains of treasure. Ha, the gold and jewels! And so many slaves . . . But Darius himself escaped me, so I pursued him east toward India. We won battle after battle as we entered strange new lands.

Q. Is it true that you never lost a battle?

A. Yes, it is true. I was wounded many times, and we endured some long sieges against strong fortresses. We fought armies of monstrous elephants at times, but my men always remained loyal because I led by example, leading the fight. They love that.

Q. So it's quiet here in Babylon. No wars seem to be going on. Why are you here?

A. Hmmm, that question I DO NOT LIKE! The men are homesick. They say they're exhausted, the weaklings. They want to see their children and wrinkled parents back in Greece. So we are heading back west. I wanted to go on into India! I still have Arabia to conquer! I am only 32. I am the master of the chariot, the long spear, the javelin, the bow, the cavalry charge . . . I am the son of ZEUS! I will never be beaten!

Q. Gulp, um, isn't Zeus just, y'know, a myth? A god in stories?

A. You think I'm crazy? The Persians know I'm not. I wear their clothes and follow their customs because it wins them over. I am *The Great* for many reasons. But now I grow weary.

Well, uh, great! Thank you for the chat. I'll give Her Majesty your regards.

Goodbye Alex

What happened next?

- Alexander became unwell when in Babylon, and he died in 323 BCE.
- Some people claim he was poisoned; others say he died of a fever.
- His body was put in a gold coffin filled with honey and taken to a huge tomb in Alexandria.
- Alexander's giant empire soon fell apart without his leadership.

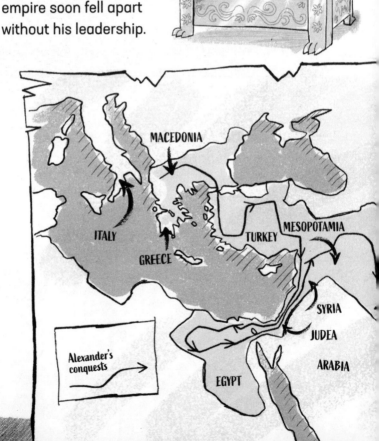

Alexander's conquests →

MACEDONIA

ITALY

GREECE

TURKEY

MESOPOTAMIA

SYRIA

JUDEA

ARABIA

EGYPT

Great facts

Alexander changed the world in just 12 years. Here are some of the things he did:

- Led his army 11,000 miles
- Founded over 70 cities
- Named a town after his horse
- Read a lot to make himself smart
- Inspired the Romans to build a huge empire like his.

Take that!

Here are just some of the lands Alexander conquered:
Anatolia (Turkey) · Syria · Judea
Egypt · Mesopotamia · Persia

PERSIA

INDIA

An interview with
Boudicca

The tranimalator has whisked me back to the year 60 CE to a corner of Iron Age Britain to meet one of history's most daring and admired women. This is going to be AMAZING.

Q. Um, can you smell something burning?
A. Yes, we've had a little bonfire.

Q. Ooh excellent—any marshmallows? I guess not from your blank look. So what were you burning? Some old woodworking projects for school? Some yard waste?
A. London.

Q. What! Huh? Actually, looking around, those do look like the charred remains of buildings. This is LONDON?
A. Was. It's just a pile of smoking rubble now, I'm pleased to say. Anyway, who exactly are you?

Q. OK, *here's the awkward part . . .* Er, I am a traveler from a distant land. Well, actually this land, but, um, another part of it. Less on fire. Can I ask you some questions please, Queen Boudicca?

A. Your dress is very unkempt. Are you a druid, or some kind of mystic? A seer perhaps?

Q. A seed actually. Anyway, what is your tribe doing in London? I thought the Iceni were from Norfolk? You know, East Anglia?

A. I do not know that name but yes, we are from north and east of here. We came to this city to destroy it.

Q. You've certainly done that! So why exactly did you burn London?

A. It's a Roman town and I hate the Romans. I really **REALLY** hate them! I want to MANGLE every last one of them!

Q. I get the picture, you're not a fan. But why?

A. Has anyone ever stolen *your* home? Has anyone taken your own land away from you? Have you been whipped and humiliated in front of your own people? Have you seen your children tortured or your friends treated like slaves? Have you been invaded, conquered, lied to, tricked, and brutalized?

Q. Um, that's no, no, no, no, no, no, no, yes, yes, and no. So what happened?

A. For centuries we Iceni ruled our corner of Britain. Yes, we occasionally had fights with the other Celtic tribes around us, but we were strong and smart. We were skilled metalworkers in gold, silver, and iron; fine weavers and woodworkers. We farmed our rich land and kept animals. We feasted with music and poetry. Our land was ours until that fateful day . . .

Q. Oh no, did you run out of woad (see page 41)?

A. There were rumors of approaching calamity. Other tribes to the south told us of a great invading army of soldiers with red shields and glinting armor. They were heading north, our way, and they appeared unstoppable.

Q. Oh, the *Romans* . . . Did you fight them?

A. The king, my husband Prasutagus, was wise. Even though we Iceni had many brave warriors and forts and chariots, we knew this army could defeat us. They were disciplined and heavily armored. They had great catapults that could demolish our defenses, and they were battle-hardened killers too—they'd crushed all the tribes to the south.

Q. So what did the king do?

A. He made a peace treaty with the Roman leaders. We agreed not to fight them—we would be on their side and follow their laws. It was the only way for us to keep our land and maintain peace.

Q. Did the plan work? I think your man was a wise dude.

A. It did at first. But the Romans taxed us and took most of the riches that the land produced. Things began to go sour . . .

Q. Yuck, no one likes sour. So where is the king now? Having a snooze? Doing a little fishing on the Thames? Torching some more Roman temples maybe?

A. He's dead.

Q. Ah, sorry. Whoops. Did the Romans do that?

A. No, he'd been ill for some time. But the Romans used the situation all right. My husband had to leave his kingdom to someone. He left half of it to Emperor Nero and half to his daughters.

Q. Ah well, your tribe got fifty percent at least, that's better than nothing, isn't it?

A. They took it all.

Q. What, your daughters did? Kids can be so annoying at times . . .

A. No, THE ROMANS! They marched in and had me flogged in front of the Iceni elders. They did much worse to others too. They stole the land that had been ours for generations. Retired Roman soldiers kicked our people out of their homes and farms and said they were theirs now. They called us captives and slaves. Do you see why we were full of fury?

Q. I do, that makes me SPIT. So how come you are here now, in smoldering London?

A. The Romans had underestimated me. They thought, "Huh, she's just a harmless woman." But I am a QUEEN, a WARRIOR QUEEN who can command horses and ride a chariot as well as any man. I wanted revenge, so I waited for my moment, and it came.

Q. Ooh, tell me more. This is better than *Spiderman III*. What happened?

A. The Romans' thirst to conquer is their weakness. Their armies spread out over Britain. Their commander Suetonius sent the main force of soldiers west to fight the Welsh.

Q. Sue who? So they had a girl in charge too?

A. Suetonius is a man, you traveling twit. While he was far away with his legions, I gathered together my Iceni and called warriors from other Celtic tribes to join us. We formed a mighty force of 120,000. We descended on their capital, Colchester, and burned it, butchering the former soldiers who lived there. The Romans were powerless to stop us with our vast numbers. Then we came here to destroy London.

Q. Did you know there's a big statue of you in London now? And there are movies about you and plays and books. You're a historical hero, a role model, a symbol of women's strength!

A. What's a book?

Q. Ah, forgot myself for a moment there . . . So what's your next move? More rebellion?

A. More burning, I guess. I think we'll do St. Albans next.

Good, I was once served some stale toast there. So what if . . . oh, she's gone.

That's revolting

What happened next?

- Boudicca's army did burn St. Albans but, meanwhile, news of the revolt had reached Suetonius.
- The Emperor Nero ordered him to end the revolt, so he gathered as many Roman forces as possible. His legions marched toward London and met Boudicca's Britons in battle.
- The Iceni were defeated by the highly trained Romans despite having much greater numbers.
- One Roman writer said Boudicca killed herself to avoid being captured. We don't know for sure.

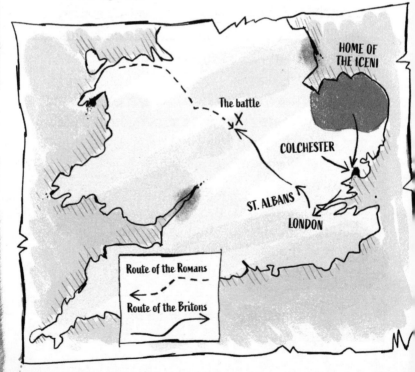

HOME OF THE ICENI

The battle
X

COLCHESTER

ST. ALBANS

LONDON

Route of the Romans

Route of the Britons

True or false?

There is very little evidence to prove what Boudicca was really like. We have to rely on the writings of two Roman historians—and some of their "facts" don't agree! She may have . . .

● Been tall
● Had long red hair
● Looked fearsome (it's thought her tribe painted themselves with blue dye from a plant called woad)
● Made big speeches to inspire her forces
● Had a different name (NO ONE agrees on the spelling).

Bring in the builders

The Romans rebuilt London and the other towns that Boudicca wrecked, adding all kinds of things, some of which are still standing today:
sturdy houses · roads · temples · drains · baths sports arenas

An interview with

Harald
Bluetooth

I've set the tranimalator for the year 980 and the land
of Norway, ready to meet . . . a Viking king!

Q. Ooh, nice longhouse. Is it all right if I sit down?
A. Who are you? Or *what* are you, more like? Those
    clothes are so strange. Are you a wolf disguised in
    human form? Have you come to speak of my fate?

Q. *I knew I shouldn't have worn this purple jacket with*
    brown pants . . . Uh, I am a traveler from a distant
    future. I won't bother explaining the whole time-
    travel thing. Is this oaken bench free?

A. Maybe you are Loki, the trickster, using your wicked magic to appear as a simple buffoon. I have my spear ready, whatever you are!

Q. Uh, I come in peace, don't shoot. I'd just like to ask you a few questions. Is that OK? My name is Andy, by the way.

A. Ah, you have riddles to ask me? Good, I like riddles! Go on.

Q. Why are you called Bluetooth?

A. Easy one. I have a dead molar, look.

Q. Oh yes, eewww, though it's more dark and yucky than blue. Harald Deadtooth doesn't sound as good, though. Anyway, did you know that we named a wireless technology after you?

A. You called it Harald? What in Odin's name is "wireless technology"?

Q. It's a thing we use in the future to watch kitten videos. Bluetooth brings devices together—I read somewhere that it was named after you because you brought together the tribes of Denmark.

A. Gah, you really do speak in riddles, Anders. But it is true, I did unite the tribes of Denmark. That is why I am the first true king of the Danes.

Q. So if you're King of Denmark, why are we in Norway?

A. Well, we are having a little trouble with our unruly German neighbors, the Saxons. Even though I built forts and ditches around the border, their armies threaten us because they have greater numbers. But since I am now King of Norway as well as Denmark, I am putting together a mighty Viking force that will allow us to defend our lands.

Q. Um, according to my elementary school teacher Mrs. Blister, Vikings were fierce warriors . . . but you look quite, uh, *mature*. Do Norsemen do retirement?

A. I may be 70 but I am still strong! My father the king lived to a great age—that is why he was called Gorm the Old.

Q. Great name! When he died, were the people sad that they were Gormless? *Ooh, I probably shouldn't have said that . . .*

A. Do not insult my father! I can pin you to the wall with this spear at any moment. My parents were mighty leaders—that is why I put up a great rune stone in their honor in Denmark. Wait, you said you are from the future—tell me, are the Jelling Stones still standing?

Q. According to Vikipedia, they are not only still there, but it's now a UNESCO World Heritage Site. We love you in the 2020s! But anyhow, about the Vikings. Is it true you are skilled sailors as well as fighters?

A. We are more than good sailors; we are lords of the sea! Have you seen the mighty longships out there in the harbor? Every month Viking merchants return to these shores with treasures from far distant lands: wine, silks, glass, spices, gold, and silver! We are explorers and great traders as well as warriors. I myself traveled far when I was younger. Where are you from?

Q. Cheadle. Uh, it's one of the top citadels in the UK. Oh, you look blank . . . Uh, Britain? Nope. England?

A. Ah, the land of the Angles? I have sailed across the western sea to Northumbria. Ha, we came back with rich pickings from the monasteries. Those monks are USELESS in a battle.

Q. Ah, yes, I can picture that . . . So you didn't consider settling in Angleland?

A. Some of my men did. They took their families there because the farmland is so rich. Here there is so little land on which to grow crops or raise animals. They love the meat and wheat over there. We do have to eat a LOT of fish here . . .

Q. So there are Vikings living in my country right now? I might go and take a look.

A. My troublesome son thinks we should raise another great force of boats and sail over there to take over the whole island, but their Saxon king, Alfred, is a crafty enemy. We have enough trouble protecting Denmark.

Q. What's your son's name?

A. Sweyn Forkbeard. Some of my friends tell me he is plotting to overthrow me and become king. By Thor's hammer, blood will be shed if that is true!

Q. Ooh, juicy stuff, but I must ask another question. Aren't you Vikings now Christians?

A. I declared Denmark to be a Christian land. I had it carved into the great stone at Jelling. So, yes. I am wearing a cross—look—and I built a big church too.

Q. But you mentioned Loki earlier, and Odin and Thor. It feels like you still trust in those Norse gods rather than Christ. Am I right?

A. You ask some hard questions, future man. I was the first Viking king to be baptized. It was done by a priest named Poppo, but my people hold on to their old ways, for sure. They still believe in giants, elves, dwarves, and monsters.

Q. So why did you try to change that?

A. Some say I declared the Danes to be Christian so that the German King Otto will stop invading us from the south—he thinks everyone should follow that faith. Others say I did it to make trading easier with Christian lands, so they are not afraid of us. Some say I truly believe in this one God. I shall say no more.

Q. Right, thank you, that's, uh, totally confusing. Anyway, one last question. You seem to have a lot of slaves around here. In my time we think forcing people from other lands to be slaves is REALLY BAD. How would you like it?

A. I would HATE it. But if I don't do it to them, they might do it to me! These are cruel, hard times. Men kill for land and power and riches. Everyone does it! That is why we are warriors, still, as well as farmers and traders. You ask too many questions. This conversation is over.

OK, I was going to ask for a selfie, but I'll probably just say bye.

Naughty boy

What happened next?

- Harald Bluetooth's son Sweyn Forkbeard started a rebellion.
- Sweyn's army eventually defeated Harald, who was probably fatally wounded.
- Bluetooth died in either 985 or 986.
- Sweyn became king of the Danes, and soon after the year 1000, he invaded England.

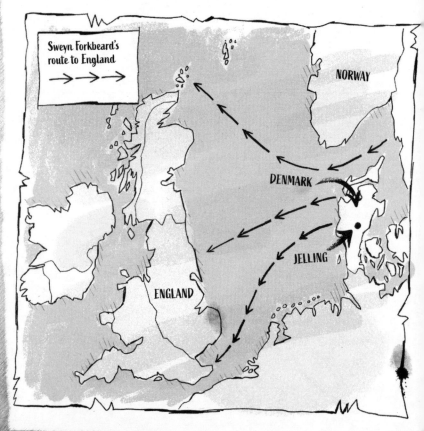

Sweyn Forkbeard's route to England

→ → →

NORWAY

DENMARK

JELLING

ENGLAND

Nifty Norse names

As well as Harald Bluetooth, Gorm the Old, and Sweyn Forkbeard, several other Viking rulers had killer names:

- Harald Greycloak
- Styrbjörn the Strong
- Eric Bloodaxe
- Ragnhild the Mighty
- Magnus the Good
- Olof the Brash

Viking beasties

Norse mythology featured some wonderful creatures, including these:

Huginn and Muninn—Odin's twin ravens that tell him what's going on in the world

Sköll—an evil wolf that chases the Sun to try and swallow it

Heidrun—a giant goat that lives on top of a huge tree and provides drinks for dead warriors from her udders

Jörmungandr—a colossal, fearsome sea serpent that encircles the realm of Midgard (the Old Norse name for Earth)

Sleipnir—a mega-speedy eight-legged horse that gets Odin around fast.

~ An interview with ~
Saladin

The tranimalator has now whizzed me back in time over 800 years to an amazing city of towers and fortresses somewhere VERY hot. I'm here to meet the legendary Crusade cruncher known as Saladin!

Q. Thank you for inviting me into your palace—very lush. You don't mind answering a few questions, do you?

A. I truly have no idea who you are, but in these lands we welcome all visitors, however, ah, *unusual* . . .

Q. Ooh, that's nice. So, um, where exactly are we?

A. This is the great city of Damascus!

Q. Ah, we're in Syria then, according to Zapp the map app. Is that right?

A. You speak in strange riddles, my friend, but yes we are in an ancient place of great importance: the Holy

Land beside us, the Turks to the north, Egypt to the west, the lands of the Arabs to the south, and Persia to the east.

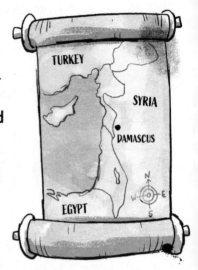

Q. **It must be busy—you should open a café! Oops, my bad, rulers don't really do that sort of thing . . . Um, is Saladin your real name?**

A. My name is Ṣalāḥ al-Dīn Yūsuf ibn Ayyūb.

Q. I think I'll just call you Saladin. Is that okay?

A. As you wish.

Q. And how would you describe yourself? King? Sultan? Chief exec? The Big S?

A. I am just a humble man of peace. A simple Kurd. A ruler, yes, but one who seeks the truth.

Q. Did you know that many people say you are one of the greatest Muslim leaders in history?

A. It does not interest me to be great. I care about doing the right thing, following God's will, and leading my people wisely.

Q. So why do you get into so many fights?

A. Why indeed? I did not seek war, it came to me.

Men arrived from afar—men with swords, wearing iron and seeking blood. They had fair skin, like you. Are you a Crusader too?

Q. No! I find metal underwear really itchy. Um, what exactly is a Crusader?

A. I see you have much to learn. The land that lies a few days south of here is no ordinary place. These are Holy Lands, sacred to Jews, Christians, and the followers of Islam, including my own people. At the heart of Palestine is the holy city of Jerusalem. Surely you have heard of that?

Q. Yes, it's in the news a lot. Go on.

A. A century ago, Muslim Turks ruled this region. They took control of Jerusalem and stopped Christian pilgrims from visiting it.

Q. Pilgrims? Who are they? Wait, you still haven't told me what Crusaders are!

A. I'm getting there. Be patient, oh pale, beardy one. Pilgrims are travelers on a journey of faith. Thousands of Christians walked to Jerusalem from their homes far away to visit the site where Jesus was crucified and buried. When they were banned, this angered the church in Rome. The Pope, Urban II, called for a special army to come over here and restore the Holy Land to Christian rule.

Q. Oh right. Well, these urban dudes have no idea what goes on out here in the country, do they . . . BUT WHO ARE THE CRUSADERS!

A. Anger is a sign of weakness. Be calm and I shall explain. Many Christian knights and men of arms from France and Germany and Italy answered the Pope's call for a War of the Cross. They journeyed here on what they thought was a holy mission, a crusade, to take back Jerusalem and the Holy Land from the Muslims.

Q. Ah right, so the Crusaders were soldiers, coming over for a scrap?

A. They were invaders. They came here to kill and occupy our lands! We were born here, our homes and families are here. We did not ask for this war! They wanted to WIPE US OUT!

Q. Calm down, anger is a sign of weakness, Mr. Saladin, tee-hee. Anyway, what happened when they came over?

A. It was, as you so artfully described, a scrap. A very bloody one. Thousands of Muslims were killed as the armored Crusaders marched toward Jerusalem. They laid siege to the city and captured it from the Turks.

Q. But all this was before your time?

A. Indeed. I was not even born then. But I know my history. We are learned people here, with many scholars. It is the way of wisdom to learn. I knew that the Christians attacked our holy Islamic temples in Jerusalem. They turned the Dome of the Rock into a church for their religion. I vowed that one day I would put things right.

Q. And did you?

A. It was my destiny. I became leader of many people– of Egyptians and Kurds and Syrians and others. I assembled an army to take back the holy city. We defeated the Crusaders at Hattin then attacked Jerusalem in 1187.

Q. I thought you said you were a man of peace?

A. I'm beginning to think you ask too many questions . . . Where is my extra-pointed mace?

Q. Oops, sorry. Carry on. You're doing a great job. What happened next?

A. The city walls were strong, and the enemy hid behind them. We laid siege but were repelled with arrows, boiling oil, and great rocks and rotting bodies thrown at us.

Q. Eeewww. What did you do?

A. I changed tactics, going for the weaker defenses. I ordered men to dig under the walls so that they collapsed. We poured in and Jerusalem was ours!

Q. Gulp, did you, uh, slaughter everyone, like in the movies?

A. I was tempted to—I cannot pretend otherwise. The Crusaders had murdered Muslims when they captured other towns. But I chose to show mercy. I let the Christians stay if they paid taxes, or leave unharmed if they wanted to. We took back control of the city and restored the Dome of the Rock on the Temple Mount. It was a glorious time.

Q. I bet it was! So, um, that was five years ago— what's going on now?

A. Alas, another Crusade has come. And this time I have a serious enemy against me . . .

Q. Ooh, some sort of dark wizard? An evil dwarf? A super-smooth villain with a cat and a death ray?

A. No, a king of England. Richard the Lionheart. He's not called that for nothing. And he has a powerful army of knights and great siege engines to hurl boulders.

Q. What will you do?

A. Pray. And hope. But I am no fool. He could take back Jerusalem, but he does not want to stay here for years guarding it. He just wants us to allow Christian pilgrims to visit the holy places once more. I will allow that. I will talk to him about it in secret and hope he will then return to England. But now I must go. I am hungry.

Q. Are you going to get the salad in, hehe?

A. Oh, HILARIOUS.

So long Saladin

What happened next?

- King Richard returned to Europe after he agreed a deal with Saladin to open Jerusalem to Christian travelers.
- Saladin died of a fever in Damascus in 1193, just a year later.
- The Crusades continued for almost 100 years as control of the Holy Land changed hands.
- The Crusaders learned much from Saladin and other Muslims about food, medicine, science, and more.

Mr. Nice Guy

Saladin is famous for the many good things he did as a ruler, such as these:

- Treating lots of prisoners well, especially women and children
- Allowing pilgrims of all faiths to visit Jerusalem
- Bringing together many tribes, peoples, and groups who once fought each other
- Being generous, giving away much of his money to the poor.

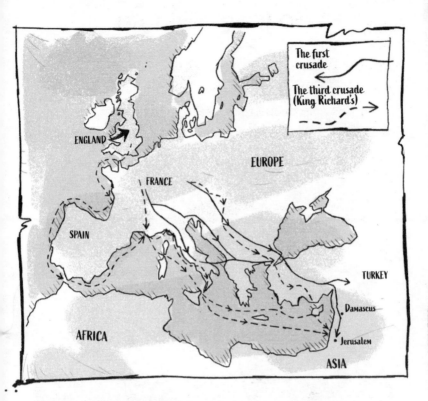

The first
crusade

The third crusade
(King Richard's)

ENGLAND

EUROPE

FRANCE

SPAIN

TURKEY

Damascus

AFRICA

Jerusalem

ASIA

Crazy Crusade?

Historians believe there was a Crusade of Children in the year 1212!

- They came from France and Germany.
- Thousands of kids joined in.
- Most of them didn't get very far and went home instead.
- No one knows for sure what really happened, but some may have died.
- It was probably NOT a good idea.

An interview with

Genghis Khan

I'm now back in the year 1222, in the remote Asian city of Karakorum, to talk to someone who was probably the most successful military commander of all time. He's a man you don't want to mess with, the Mongol Monster himself . . . Mister Genghis Khan!

Q. Hi, are you well? Nice yurt you have here.
A. Uh, you must be the shaman that my advisers told me about.

Q. I don't think so. Not a shaman, no. I applied to be a mailman once, though. Uh, what is a shaman?
A. A holy man—a guide who speaks to the spirit world through a trance. I met one once who told me that

the whole surface of the world would be mine. Yet I am getting old and there is still much to conquer. Hmph, I was hoping you would be the one to see into my future.

Q. Well, as it happens, I am from the future! It's your lucky day. All you have to do is answer a few questions and I will reveal the mysteries of tomorrow, haha.

A. That is good—I was about to have you boiled alive. Perhaps you possess the elixir of everlasting life? The monks claim there is no such thing . . . Anyway, tell me, what does the future hold? Are there still warriors on horseback in your time? Which mighty chieftains rule the land? Do you live in a great palace? I am eager to know.

Q. Good! Well, I actually live in an old Victorian house with a leaky roof. And I definitely wouldn't call our current leaders mighty—they're more kind of mushy. We still have horses, but there's been a serious warrior shortage for years. We spend most of our time looking at WhatsApp and trying to find a parking space. Anyhoo, is Genghis your real name?

A. Are you *sure* you aren't a shaman? You speak the same kind of nonsense. Since you ask, my real name is Temüjin.

Q. Well, I was in a trance watching a soccer game last week . . . Oh, right, so why did your name change?

A. The answer is part of my story. I was born here in the wild mountains of Mongolia, into a tribe of nomads. My father was the leader of our clan, but he was poisoned by a rival tribe when I was just nine. On that day I vowed revenge.

Q. That's tough when you're just a little kid. What happened next?

A. With my brothers I learned how to survive and grow up. We were poor but brave and cunning. I grew big and strong. I needed help to defeat my enemies, so I went to the chief of another tribe—one of my father's allies—to ask for help. He took me in and later I married his daughter, Börte. She was a true princess.

Q. So things started to go well?

A. For a while. Until another group of Mongols, the Merkits, raided our camp and stole her away.

Q. Yikes! She was kidnapped?

A. Yes. To get her back I had to become more than just a fighter. I had to become a leader–to gather strong men around me who would follow me. That is what I did. I built an army of trustworthy warriors, and we killed the Merkits and rescued Börte.

Q. Nice work! So how did all this lead to a name change?

A. There is much still to tell. I saw how my marriage had united our two tribes and made us all stronger. The many Mongol tribes were always battling and stealing from each other. I realized that if I brought them all together we could be a mighty people. Then we could stand up to the Chinese, who always managed to control us.

Q. Ah, you're a man with a plan. But how did you do it?

A. I married more women who were daughters of chieftains. I brought the tribes of Mongolia together, and I became their sole ruler.

Q. Wow, that's a lot of weddings to organize–you must be good at speeches. So was that when your name changed?

A. Indeed. In the year 1206 the clan leaders declared me to be Genghis Khan, which means "emperor of all."

Q. OK, so at that point, you're the Daddy, the Big Boss. What did you do with your sparkly new empire?

A. I see you are one of limited understanding . . . I will explain. Mongolia was now a great nation. Before this it was just a poor, mountainous land of squabbling tribes. Now we were a threat to the other kingdoms around us—we were powerful and they wanted to stop us.

Q. I am not very familiar with the empires of 13th century Asia, that's true. So what did you do?

A. I got to work building the army. We Mongols are supreme horse riders and archers, but I made us even better. Then we invaded the smaller kingdoms around us. Nothing could stop us. But we gave them a choice—either join us or we obliterate you.

Q. Gulp. Did it work?

A. Of course. Our Mongol Empire became larger and stronger. Most of them joined us, and I gave every loyal man a fair chance to rise up and become an officer. I believed in rewarding ability. We would need that to defeat our greatest enemy.

Q. What, fear?

A. No, you fool, China.

Q. Oh, yes, China. I knew that. Did you invade them as well?

A. By this time, I had seen the strength of our huge numbers and our discipline. The campaign was planned in fine detail. We had a strategy and we had POWER.

Q. But, um, how did you get over the wall?

A. The wall?

Q. Yes, the Great Wall of China. That really, really big stone thing.

A. Oh that. We marched around it.

Q. What! Can you do that?

A. Yes, they left a gap at the end. We laid waste to towns and burned villages, and our vast Mongol hordes descended on their capital, the great city of Beijing.

Q. Ah, where they had the Olympics?

A. Whatever. The walled city was defended by huge battlements, so we laid siege and let the people starve. They hurled pots of burning oil and waste at us, but we held back until they were weak.

Q. Waste? You mean like old baked bean cans and molded bread?

A. I mean POOP! Anyway, we took the city and slaughtered the inhabitants. A great victory!

Q. Ah yes, I wanted to ask you about the whole, um, death thing.

A. Death?

Q. You know, the endless killing. The mass murder? According to books I've read, your armies caused the death of over ten million people! Writers mention pyramids of skulls. Why so much blood and gore? Isn't all that a bit, you know, *mean*?

A. Weaklings like you will never understand. I rule the largest empire the world has ever seen! After defeating the Chinese, my armies went west and crushed all before them: Afghanistan, Persia, Azerbaijan, Southern Russia, Georgia, and on into Europe: Bulgaria and Hungary. You cannot invade that many lands without bloodshed! In fact, annoying traveler, I might just add one more to the numbers . . .

Q. Sorry, uh, no I think you're GREAT. It's just the books that say you were a cruel, violent ruler who showed no mercy.

A. Listen, NO ONE had heard of the Mongols before me. I made them feared and famous. But I also made laws and brought new ideas to many lands and increased trade and wealth. I am not all bad . . . So back to the future . . . You will now give me the elixir of everlasting life and tell me when I will conquer the rest of the world. Or else.

OK, I just need to head back to the future to get that stuff from the store—won't be a sec. Go tranimalator, GO!

Oh yes I Khan

What happened next?

- The Mongol Empire continued to grow, as nothing could stop its army of 200,000 soldiers.
- Genghis Khan was ruthless in dealing with enemies—he had rival rulers crushed to death.
- He died suddenly in 1227 in China, some believe after falling from his horse.
- His four sons continued to rule most of Asia, conquering more lands and destroying cities.

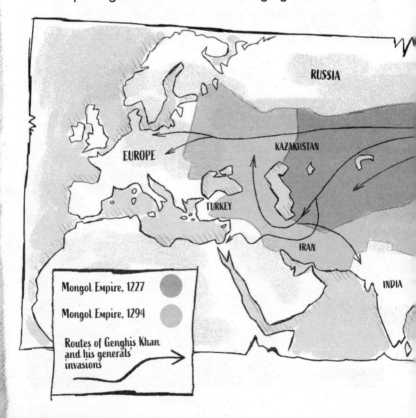

RUSSIA

EUROPE

KAZAKHSTAN

TURKEY

IRAN

INDIA

Mongol Empire, 1227

Mongol Empire, 1294

Routes of Genghis Khan and his generals' invasions

Local hero

Genghis Khan struck fear around the world, but in Mongolia he is honored as a hero:

- His name and picture are on paper money, drinks, food labels, and more
- The country's main airport is named after him
- People recognize that he brought great wealth and new inventions to a poor country
- His secret place of burial has never been discovered, but there are statues of him.

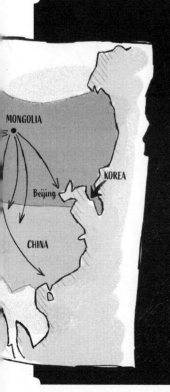

How big?

Asia is the world's biggest continent, but Genghis Khan ruled most of it in the 1200s:

- At its largest, the Mongol Empire covered 12 million square miles
- It was twice as big as the massive Roman Empire
- It would take a year to walk from end to end
- GK had so many wives and children that historians think 16 million living people are descended from him!

An interview with
Mansa Mūsā

Oh wow, I am now on the edge of the mighty Sahara desert in West Africa. It is the year 1331 and I am only going to have a convo with the RICHEST MAN IN HISTORY, that's all!

Q. Hello Mansa Mūsā, your mighty majesty! Um, where exactly are we?

A. Welcome, my tall, pink friend. You are our esteemed guest here in my palace in the great city of Timbuktu.

Q. Right, nice. Which country are we in?

A. You are here and yet you don't know where you are? You are indeed a most mysterious traveler. But, anyway, this is the great kingdom of Mali.

Q. Yes, sorry, I've been to so many places now that I'm getting muddled. Anyway, shall I call you Mansa or Mūsā or M&M or sir . . .?

A. I am Mūsā I, Mansa of the Mali Empire. Mansa means sultan or king if you like. You can call me Emperor.

Q. Ah right, got it. So is it true?

A. What?

Q. Are you the richest dude in history? Mr. Moneybags? The original trillionaire?

A. Ah, so this is why you have come here . . . In Mali we are blessed with much gold, it is true. My most learned scholars at the university here tell me that I possess half the world's gold, and yet it is not important to me.

Q. Well, if *you* don't want it . . . ha, just kidding. So what is important to you?

A. I am a devout Muslim, a man of faith. What matters to me is to do the will of the Almighty.

Q. Ah, that's why there are lots of mosques here! But, um, if you are so wealthy, how come your palace and so much of this city is made of MUD?

A. A choice question, Mr. Indy. Some of the buildings contain stone, but here earth is the traditional building material. Mixed with straw, it dries hard in the desert heat and makes sturdy walls, which also help keep us cool.

Q. It's Andy, actually.

A. Yes, it's very handy—we couldn't manage without mud.

Q. So, anyway, I read that you went on a totally EPIC journey. Is that right?

A. Ah, you must be referring to my hajj. Every Muslim has a duty to travel to the holy city of Mecca in Arabia once in his lifetime. Mine took over a year and was a 6,400-kilometre trek across the mighty Sahara by caravan.

Q. What! You went in a VAN? Surely the richest emperor can travel in something fancier than a van!

A. Hmm, your mind is a festival of confusion, my friend. A caravan is a traveling procession of people and animals. I was accompanied by 60,000—a veritable walking city!

Q. Whoa, that's like going on a road trip with a small city! Who were they?

A. My family of royals, plus officials, soldiers, merchants, entertainers, camel drivers, slaves, and others.

Q. Um, why did you take so many people?

A. Mali was an unknown kingdom, a backwater, a place few had even heard of. I wished to put it on the map and bring visitors and trade here. But to do so I had to be generous.

Q. What, you took presents along, you mean?

A. Every one of my 12,000 slaves carried a bag of gold weighing four pounds. It was given to the poor we met along the way. I made great gifts to every city we visited.

Q. Woah, I bet everyone LOVED meeting you . . .

A. Indeed, I was somewhat popular on that journey. But more importantly, those we met learned quickly that Mali was not some backward outpost—it was a mighty kingdom, the richest in all the Earth!

Q. Right, I see your plan. You put on a big show and splashed the cash to bring people here. A tourist boom, was it?

A. The people who came were not on vacation, oh simple one. They were traders who brought beautiful and useful things and new foods from distant places. But also, people came here to learn.

Q. You have schools here? In the Middle Ages?

A. Of course! As well as mosques, I built the great University of Sankore and a vast library. Astronomers and mathematicians and other wise scholars came here to study.

Q. So you put the gold to good use—good job. What's your next plan?

A. I must build better walls and forts to protect the city from invaders. Those from the lands around are greedy to lay their hands on our riches. But my greatest foe is the desert. Every day it threatens to swallow us with storms of sand.

Q. Well, as my granny used to say, you can't win 'em all. Thank you for the interview. Um, any spare gold on hand before I go?

A. I think not.

Mali messes up

What happened next?

- Mūsā died a few years later, and his sons wasted his great wealth.
- Timbuktu eventually lost its status as a rich trading city.
- The Sahara desert did bury some of the streets, but the city survives.
- Mūsā's university and many of his earth buildings are still standing today.

The mud mosque

Mansa Mūsā's Djinguereber Mosque has survived in the desert for almost 800 years:

- It was built in 1327.
- An architect traveled from Spain to create it.
- He was paid with 440 lb of gold.
- The mosque is now a World Heritage Site.
- The mud walls sometimes have to be repaired after heavy rains.

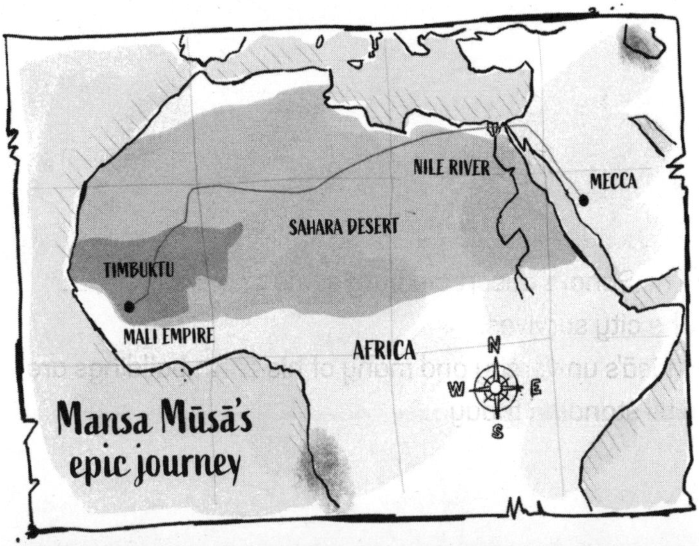
NILE RIVER
MECCA
SAHARA DESERT
TIMBUKTU
MALI EMPIRE
AFRICA
N
W
E
S
Mansa Mūsā's epic journey

Mysterious Timbuktu

Here are some reasons why this small remote city is famous:

Myth or real?–some people still believe the city does not exist (it does!)

Hot, hot, hot–summer temperatures in the city are too high for most people

A buried city–desert sand covers the streets and buildings of the town

Tough travel–it's a very hard place to reach, even today, with only dirt roads in and out

It's in a saying–'From here to Timbuktu' means reaching somewhere far away.

An interview with
Montezuma

The tranimalator has now pinged me over to a startling city built on a lake island, high in the mountains of Mexico. Yes, I'm here in the year 1520 to meet the ruler of the mighty AZTECS no less!

Q. Hi Mr. Montezuma, how are you doing?
A. Hmmm . . . What?

Q. You do seem a little, uh, distracted. Does it have anything to do with all these soldiers around here?
A. Sshhhh, they'll hear you!

Q. Oh, sorry, is that bad? I mean you're their boss and everything, aren't you? Actually, they look and sound kind of Spanish.
A. That is because they are Spanish!

Q. So, um, why are there Spanish guards in your palace? I mean, as Emperor of the Aztecs shouldn't you have, like, Aztec henchman around? I would.

A. Good question. It's kind of awkward . . .

Q. Go on, tell me! Awkward is good. Awkward is interesting. Is it something juicy?

A. It's a long story . . . Ah well, I don't suppose I am going anywhere soon, so I might as well tell you. So who exactly are you?

Q. My name is Andy and I'm an enormously popular children's author from the 21st century. I'm buzzin' around through time asking big shot rulers all the questions!

A. What? You expect me to believe that!

Q. What, that I'm from the future?

A. No, that you're popular. Anyway, how is the world different in your time?

Q. Well, it's more kind of *digital*. And noisy. And pizza-y!

A. Our ancient writings foretold that strange creatures would appear in the years to come, but I didn't think they would be *this* weird. Anyway, my story. Three years ago, some of my people came with reports of white men with great boats landing on the coast many miles to the east.

Q. Oh, the conquistadors?

A. I do not know that word. But anyway, they set off in this direction with their horses, armor, and heavy weapons. They arrived here last year.

Q. Ooh, did you fight them?

A. No, I welcomed them. We outnumbered them by far, and anyway I wanted to know who these foreigners were with their crossbows and cannons and mysterious language. I found someone who could translate. We learned they came from a land far across the great ocean, called Spain.

Q. I've been there on vacation. The ice cream was fantastic. Oh, sorry, what happened next?

A. I gave them gifts and welcomed them as guests in my palace. They were friendly and said they did not want trouble. Their leader was a man named Hernán Cortés. He seemed very interested in where we obtained our gold.

Q. Did you tell him?

A. Of course not. I am no fool! I told him about the strength of our empire, about our markets full of objects made by skilled craftsmen. I hoped they would trade with us. But he just asked a lot of questions. He wanted to know about the various buildings here in Tenochtitlán.

Q. Yes, what *are* those tall stone things with lots of steps?

A. Not YOU as well . . . Those are temples. We Aztecs worship many gods. It is important to please them.

Q. So what happened next with your visitors?

A. One day, without warning, Cortés told me I could not leave this house. His soldiers guarded every entrance. I found myself a prisoner in my own palace! I should never have trusted the Spaniards . . .

Q. Oh heck! What are you going to do? Look, I live 500 years from now and one thing I have learned is that PANICKING DOESN'T WORK!

A. I haven't finished yet—things got worse. Yesterday there was a big festival in the city to honor one of the most important gods. The Spaniards were fretting because there were so many people out in the street. A huge crowd gathered by the temple—the soldiers must have thought the people were massing to fight them.

Q. But you weren't?

A. No! But the Spaniards saw that many nobles were gathered in the temple, so they went there with weapons and butchered them! A cruel massacre. And I was trapped in here, powerless . . . The people are furious, they think I am on the side of the enemy.

Q. What will you do now?

A. I must convince Cortés to let me speak to the people, to explain that I have been a hostage, and to tell them that I wanted peace with the Spanish to protect our beautiful city of Tenochtitlán. But wait—if you can travel through time, you can go a few days into the future and then come back and tell me what happens! Can you? Will you? I will give you many rewards.

Q. OK, sounds like a plan. I'll just zip two days forward, then be right back in a flash. All right?

A. Yes, go! Go! Oh, he's gone. It must work–amazing! My word, he's back already! What did you find?

Um, ooh, how can I put this . . .? Uh . . . Oh, everything's FINE. Gotta dash now, bye!

Montezuma's missile

What happened next?

- Montezuma tried to speak to the Aztecs, but they were furious and threw rocks at him.
- It is thought that he was hit by one of these and died.
- The Aztecs rose up and drove the Spanish soldiers out, but they returned with a bigger army.
- The Spaniards defeated the Aztecs and took over their empire and the land around it.

High-tech trouble

So how did a small army of Europeans defeat a huge number of warriors?

- They had much stronger and better weapons.
- The Aztecs did not have the technology to make crossbows, cannons, and guns.
- The Spanish were helped by nearby tribes who were enemies of the Aztecs.
- The invaders unknowingly brought diseases such as smallpox, which killed thousands of local people.

Remains of Tenochtitlán

Mexico City was built over the ancient capital, but lots of evidence has been found of:

Temples—where worship was carried out, plus animal and human sacrifices

Palaces—where the nobles lived

Sports grounds—the Aztecs played ball games

Gardens—only for the rich

Zoos—for Montezuma's own collection of beasts.

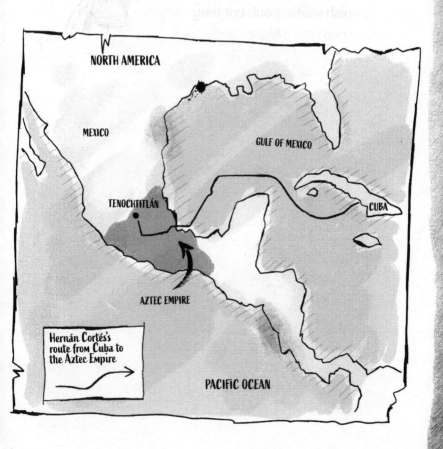

NORTH AMERICA

MEXICO

GULF OF MEXICO

TENOCHTITLÁN

CUBA

AZTEC EMPIRE

Hernán Cortés's route from Cuba to the Aztec Empire

PACIFIC OCEAN

An interview with

Elizabeth I

Well, it's exciting to be back now in England, in the year 1601. I'm in a big palace on the bank of the River Thames and I am about to have a chat with one of the country's greatest monarchs ever. Bring it on!

Q. An honor to meet you, Your Queenly Tudor Majesty! So the big question is, hands for feet or feet for hands?

A. Are you unwell? I do not understand your jabbering at all.

Q. Sorry, it's a sort of fun party-game-ice-breaker-thing. I meant if you had to choose, would you rather have hands where you have feet or feet where your hands are . . . Perhaps that wasn't such a good question after all?

A. Indeed. You are wasting my time, whoever you are.

Q. Right, fair point. Can you tell me about your early life? Being a princess and all that?

A. My childhood was no fairy tale. I may have been the daughter of the king, Henry VIII, but I had more stepmothers than fingers on my right hand! I suppose that I was lucky to have been too young to remember my mother having her head removed.

Q. Ugh! OK, let's change the subject. So you became queen in your twenties?

A. A long time ago that seems! Many powerful people thought I would be a weak ruler, easily manipulated, but I have proved them wrong. My father may have been cruel, but he gave me something more valuable than these glinting jewels on my necklace.

Q. What, a top-of-the-range Porsche?

A. Pardon?

Q. Oh no, cars haven't been invented yet, my bad. Um, a golden castle?

A. The finest teachers in the land! Many say I am the best educated woman alive. I speak four languages and know about politics, art, philosophy, and more. Who exactly *are* you, anyway?

Q. Me? Oh, a mere writer who wishes to, uh, pen great things about England's Good Queen Bess.

A. Hmm, then why are you dressed like a theatrical buffoon?

Q. Hey, in my town this is considered stylish. Anyway, what's it like being a royal sovereign ruler?

A. Ha, people think it's all palaces and wealth and feasts and being served night and day and having silk dresses, but the truth is dark and frightening.

My life is full of plots and danger and rebellion. I am constantly surrounded by people who want power—rivals and hangers-on and greedy, ambitious men.

Q. Isn't *anyone* helpful?

A. I have my trusted advisers, led by Robert Cecil, and my network of spies, so I know what is going on. I try to be a good and wise queen for ordinary people too, but it is hard. They want me to be strong and win victories over our enemies, Spain and France, but they don't want to pay taxes for ships and soldiers. They want cheap food, but I cannot control the weather that decides the harvests. Life is impossible most of the time—I don't know how I have stayed on the throne for 42 years . . .

Q. 42 years! You must have a really sore bottom!

A. So, anyway, you are a writer, you say. Are you like William Shakespeare, my favorite playwright?

Q. Um, cough, yes, *kind* of like him, sure. We both have beards. But can I ask you why you never married. Don't you want an heir—a son or daughter to succeed you as king or queen?

A. Oh I HATE that question! Why are people so obsessed with my having a husband? I have chosen not to. I am a strong, independent and capable monarch—I don't need a man to help me rule!

Q. OK, I get the picture. Have you had any offers, though?

A. ANY OFFERS? Hundreds of men have asked to marry me! THE NERVE! I should have you thrown in the Tower. Huh, as well as from half the lords and knights of this country, I have had proposals from royal princes in Sweden, Austria, Denmark, Spain, and more. Even Ivan the Terrible of Russia popped the question.

Q. Good thing you didn't marry him—you'd be Elizabeth the Terrible. What a silly name. Aren't there any guys with good names like Brian the Brilliant or Frank the Fab?

A. I shall ignore that. Of course, I know marrying into one of Europe's royal families is the done thing—it forms alliances and helps to maintain peace, but I am too old now anyway. So where's my gift, mister writer?

Q. Gift?

A. Yes, it is usual for all visitors to bring me something—a present. Sometimes it is a simple ruby or precious fur, but others make more effort. Francis Drake brought me new lands, gold, and victory against the Spanish. Walter Raleigh came with the delicious potato and valuable tobacco. What have you brought?

Q. Ooh, uh, let me have a look in my pockets . . . I've got two fluffy peppermints and a used bus ticket. Any good?

A. Servants! Throw this man in jail!

Q. Wait, isn't that whole Walter Raleigh thing a myth? Didn't potatoes first come here from Spain?

A. DON'T MENTION THE SPANISH TO ME! Someone call the executioner!

Q. I take it you're not a big fan of Spain?

A. NO I AM NOT. They are behind all of the Catholic plots to remove me as queen because I am a Protestant. And anyway, they did try to invade this country in 1588. Even you must have heard of the Armada?

Q. Yes, we did learn about that in school. King Philip II of Spain sent 130 ships full of soldiers, didn't he?

A. He did, but we defeated him! My loyal sailors helped me win a great victory.

Q. Oh right. I thought they were beaten because the wind blew their sailing ships in the wrong direction. And they were hit by storms. Hey, anyway, wasn't there an English Armada that failed to conquer Spain too?

A. You really are determined to DIE. Executioner, bring your axe—the really blunt one.

Q. Wait! I need to ask you why your skin is lumpy. Is that because you had smallpox? And some of your teeth are missing—I read that's because you eat so many sweets. Is that true? And I haven't asked you yet why you had Mary, Queen of Scots's head chopped off.

A. Hold on, executioner. This fool may be asking for torture and death, but I cannot deny he's brave. No one else has dared mention my rotten teeth before. Perhaps he could be useful to me as a spy, especially as he managed to sneak into the palace unnoticed.

Q. Sounds fun. I could be a kind of Tudor 007: James de Bonde. What gadgets do I get?

A. If you work for me and uncover traitors and plots, then there will be rich rewards: wealth, jewels, property . . . Or perhaps you seek a title? I could make you Earl of Penge.

Q. It's a tempting offer, but I would prefer to live in a land with real toilets. Best dash.

A. EXECUTIONER!!

Liz leaves us

What happened next?

- Elizabeth reigned for two more years, but her health was in decline and she died in 1603.
- She reigned for 44 years and was popular for most of the time.
- She had no children of her own, so the throne went to the next in line, James I.
- He was king of Scotland but became an unpopular king of England.

Bring me power!

All kinds of things happened in the Elizabethan age:

- England became a world power, thanks to her success at sea
- As well as a strong navy, pirates, and explorers helped bring riches from distant lands
- Walter Raleigh and others claimed part of the New World (the Americas) for the queen
- Her reign was also a golden age of art, music, writing, and architecture.

SCOTLAND

IRELAND

ENGLAND

FRANCE

ATLANTIC
OCEAN

SPAIN

Route of the
Spanish Armada

Dangerous times

Elizabeth was a great ruler, but it was a bad idea
to oppose her:

- Over 400 people were executed during
  her reign
- These included many priests accused of
  holding illegal services
- Some nobles were beheaded, such as the Earl
  of Essex, and some were hanged
- Others put to death included traitors and
  women accused of witchcraft.

An interview with

Akbar the Great

My trusty tranimalator has now zapped me through time to the year 1600 to the famous city of Agra in northern India to meet another of the Greats. This time it's the awesome Akbar!

Q. Greetings, O mighty ruler . . . WAIT, you're just a KID! How old are you? 11, 12?

A. How dare you! You come here and insult me? I am the emperor of the Mughals! I could have you chopped into a thousand pieces. And anyway, I'm 13.

Q. What? Oh, sorry, your royal greatness, but I was expecting someone, um, a teensy bit older. Are you sure you're Akbar? You're very little to be ruling a whole empire.

A. YES OF COURSE I AM AKBAR!

Q. This is the year 1600, isn't it?

A. No, you oaf, it's 1556.

Q. Really? Oh, that would explain why I'm talking to the mini-Akbar! Silly tranimalator, the battery must be going. I don't suppose you have any spare triple-As, do you, Akkie?

A. Wait, am I right in thinking this strange device has transported you through time? How magical! Tell me, what does the future hold for us Mughals? I want to know if I become a mighty leader.

Q. Well, according to this history book I borrowed from Frottlepot Library, you will go on to rule most of India, Pakistan, Afghanistan, and Bangladesh. How does that sound?

A. EPIC! Good, good. I only rule a small part of India right now—tell me more!

Q. Um, let's see, well, it says here you become very rich and powerful. Happy?

A. Indeed, this is most excellent. But how do I do it?

Q. Ah, right . . . partly through strong military action, winning battles. Is that what you expected?

A. Yes! I love a good fight. What else?

Q. Also through trading with other countries—could that happen?

A. Good idea, I like it! Yes, sell some of India's finest produce and buy the things we need . . . Anything more?

Q. You also go on to keep the many conquered peoples happy by allowing them to follow their own faiths and traditions, instead of forcing your own upon them. Like that one?

A. Meh, it's alright. A bit dull. Not as good as battles and the rest.

Q. Plus, did you know that in the future you make the Mughal Empire run successfully through efficient organization and administration?

A. BORING! I am tiring of you now. Someone take this pest away.

Q. Yikes. Come on tranimalator, let's try again for 1600. Go!

A. My goodness! It's YOU! I don't believe it, you're back after 44 years!

Q. Eek, that was weird. It felt like about three seconds to me . . . Hey, everything's different . . . and you are MUCH older. You are Akbar, aren't you?

A. My friend! The Merchant of Eternity, this is a wonderful day—I have so much to tell you! Yes, indeed it is I, Akbar, emperor of the Mughal Empire, and now 58 years old. But you have not changed at all. How is this possible?

Q. Actually, I could do with a change of socks—time travel really makes your feet sweat. Anyway, what is it you want to tell me?

A. That day, when you came to visit me, all those years ago . . . I was but a child. I had been placed on the throne when my father died. I did not care for all the responsibility of that role . . . I did not understand it. Ha, I just wanted to go hunting and to feast and fight!

Q. So what happened after I, uh, left?

A. I remember the things you told me. They are burned into my mind. You said I would be the rich and powerful leader of a much larger empire, winning battles and establishing trade. You told me I would be a tolerant ruler and a shrewd organizer.

Q. Yes, so don't tell me you packed it all in and became a blogger instead?

A. It all came true. Everything you said! I mulled it over for years, and as I became older and wiser, I understood that your ideas were the only way to make an enormous kingdom work. Otherwise, people are always rebelling because they are unhappy.

Q. Ah, nice! That's why we need to value our libraries, see! So what are you up to these days?

A. I have done so much. I conquered many tribes and peoples all the way across India and beyond. They

Rule *with* Terror *in* 5 Easy Steps

Whizdom for Beginners

Book to the *Future*

are mainly Hindus, so they feared me because I am a Muslim, and my mother was Persian. But I allowed them to continue their ways and follow their faith and culture. In fact, I made many of them into important officials. I even married some of their women.

Q. Wow, you don't mess around! But you did use a lot of guns too, right?

A. Of course, I had to defeat my enemies. I bought firearms and cannons from Europe. And I used war elephants to charge and strike fear into those who opposed me. They pooped their pants! But listen,

that was mostly long ago. Now I have discovered the value of learning and understanding, and the beauty of art. I have built libraries and glorious buildings. I pay artists and craftsmen to make my cities and palaces splendid.

Q. **Yes, but is it true you threw your foster brother out a window, twice?**

A. Maybe . . . Well, he was trying to grab power!

That sounds like a yes to me. Anyway, my advice is
keep being tolerant of other people—then you'll be
remembered well. If you do, I'll return from the future
again and bring you some gummy bears. Toodle-oo.

Going big

What happened next?

What happened to the mighty Mughal Empire?

- Akbar's strategy of being a fair ruler for all his subjects helped keep the peace.
- During his rule the empire tripled in size.
- Akbar died from a disease called dysentery in 1605.
- The Mughal Empire grew even larger and lasted until the 1800s.

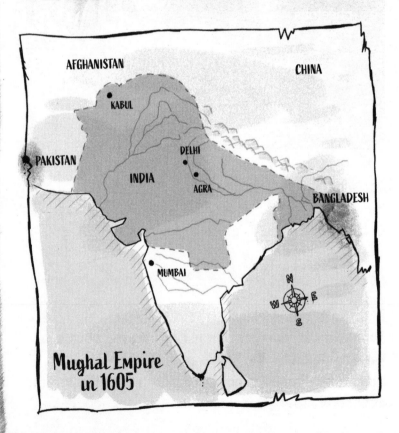

Mughal Empire in 1605

Quite a life

These are just some of the things that Akbar experienced in his lifetime:

- He was hit in the shoulder with an arrow fired by an assassin
- He was once attacked by a tiger, but survived
- He trained elephants and kept several hunting cheetahs
- He may have had as many as 300 wives
- He created a library just for women.

Mughal monarch mix

Here are some other Mughal emperors:

Babur—the empire's founder, descended from Genghis Khan

Jahāngīr—Akbar's son, whose name in Persian means "world-seizer"

Shah Jahān—the famous Taj Mahal was built in his time

Aẓam Shah—his reign lasted just three months before he was killed in battle

Bahādur Shah II—the last emperor, at the time when the British controlled India.

An interview with

Quiz

Q 1. Who did Cleopatra have to marry when she was queen of Egypt?

a. Julius Caesar ☐   b. Mark Anthony ☐

c. Her little brother ☐   d. The Sphinx ☐

Q 2. How did Cleopatra sneak into the palace to meet Julius Caesar?

a. She was rolled in a rug ☐

b. She was hidden in a pie ☐

c. She dressed as a guard ☐

d. She had herself mailed to him ☐

Q 3. What was Alexander the Great's nickname for his favorite horse?

a. Big head ☐

b. Ox head ☐

c. Cow face ☐

d. Bear bottom ☐

Q 4. Why did Alexander's army turn back in Babylon?

a. They were homesick ☐

b. They were bored ☐

c. They kept losing battles ☐

d. They ran out of bullets ☐

Q 5. What did Boudicca do when she visited London?

a. Made it her capital ☐   b. Rebuilt it ☐

c. Went to see a musical ☐   d. Burned it ☐

Q 6. What was Boudicca's tribe called?

a. the Icki ☐   b. The Iceni ☐

c. The Icing ☐   d. The Romans ☐

Q 7. What were Vikings like Harald Bluetooth particularly good at?

a. Dancing ☐

b. Making soup ☐

c. Sailing ☐

d. Tennis ☐

Q 8. What was Harald Bluetooth's father called?

a. Sweyn Forkbeard ☐

b. Gorm the Old ☐

c. Otto ☐

d. Eddie the Eagle ☐

Q 9. Which country was Genghis Khan from?

a. Mongolia ☐   b. Mali ☐

c. Madagascar ☐   d. Wales ☐

Q 10. What did the people of Beijing hurl at Genghis Khan?

a. Boulders ☐   b. Insults ☐

c. Bodies ☐   d. Poop ☐

Q 11. Mansa Mūsā was the richest man in Africa because he had lots of what?

a. Gold ☐   b. Sand ☐

c. Camels ☐   d. Hit records ☐

Q 12. Which building constructed by Mansa Mūsā in Timbuktu is still there today?

a. The mosque ☐   b. The pyramid ☐

c. The gym ☐   d. The university ☐

Q 13. Which people was Saladin famous for fighting?

a. The Saxons ☐

b. The Crusaders ☐

c. The Turks ☐

d. The Beatles ☐

Q 14. Which important city did Saladin capture in 1187?

a. Rome ☐   b. Jerusalem ☐

c. L.A. ☐   d. Moscow ☐

Q 15. Akbar the Great conquered which country?

a. India ☐ b. Japan ☐

c. Egypt ☐ d. Iceland ☐

Q 16. Which animals did Akbar use to scare his enemies?

a. Monkeys ☐ b. Tigers ☐

c. Elephants ☐ d. Hamsters ☐

Q 17. Which people did Montezuma rule?

a. The Mughals ☐ b. The Aztecs ☐

c. The Incas ☐ d. The under-fives ☐

Q 18. What were Montezuma's amazing temples made of?

a. Gold ☐

b. Wood ☐

c. Stone ☐

d. Pasta ☐

Q 19. Which people did Elizabeth I employ to find out about her rivals?

a. Spies ☐ b. Executioners ☐

c. Spaniards ☐ d. Bus drivers ☐

Q 20. What did Elizabeth I have missing?

a. Her toenails ☐ b. Her teeth ☐

c. Her ears ☐ d. Her head ☐

Glossary

amulet A small ornament or piece of jewelry thought to give protection against danger, evil, or disease.

Aristotle (384–322 BCE) Greek philosopher, pupil of Plato, and tutor of Alexander the Great.

Armada The large fleet of ships sent by Philip II of Spain in 1588 to invade Elizabeth I's England.

Aztecs The people who ruled a large empire in the 15th and early 16th centuries in what is now central and southern Mexico.

baptism A religious ceremony to admit people to Christianity.

bluetooth A short-range wireless technology that is used for exchanging data between devices over short distances.

Catholic A member of the Catholic Church and a follower of the Christian religion.

conquistador A conqueror, especially relating to any of the leaders of the Spanish conquerors of Mexico and Peru in the 16th century.

Crusades The medieval military expeditions made by Europeans to take the Holy Land from the Muslims in the 11th, 12th, and 13th centuries.

crusader A fighter in the medieval Crusades.

Dane A native or inhabitant of Denmark.

druid A priest, soothsayer, or magician in the ancient Celtic religion.

dysentery An infection of the intestines that causes severe diarrhea containing mucus or blood.

hajj The Muslim pilgrimage to the holy city of Mecca in Saudia Arabia, which all Muslims are expected to make at least once in their lifetime if they can.

Hindu A follower of Hinduism, a major religious and cultural tradition of South Asia.

Iceni A tribe of ancient Britons inhabiting an area of southeastern England (which is in present-day Norfolk and Suffolk). Their queen was Boudicca.

Iron Age A prehistoric period (from about 1100 BCE) when people began making tools and weapons out of iron.

Jelling Stones Huge carved runestones from the 10th century, erected in the town of Jelling, Denmark, by Harald Bluetooth, in memory of his parents.

Kurd A member of a mainly Islamic people living in northern Iraq, western Iran, eastern Syria, and parts of eastern Turkey.

legion A division of the ancient Roman army, made up of between 3,000–6,000 soldiers.

Loki The Norse god of mischief and destruction.

Odin In Norse mythology, the god of war and death and the supreme creator god.

pharaoh The title (meaning "great house") given to the rulers of ancient Egypt.

pilgrim A traveler on a journey of faith.

Protestant A member or follower of any of the Western Christian Churches that are separate from the Roman Catholic Church.

rune Any of the letters of an ancient Germanic alphabet used by people in northern Europe, from the 3rd century CE to the end of the Middle Ages. A rune, carved on wood or stone, was believed to have magical powers.

Saxon A member of the people who inhabited parts of northern and central Germany from Roman times. Many Saxons conquered and settled in much of southern England in the 5th and 6th centuries.

scribe A person who copies out documents.

seer A person who has supernatural insight and who can see visions of the future.

shaman A holy man or guide who speaks to the spirit world through a trance.

siege A military operation in which the enemy surrounds a town, cutting off essential supplies, with the aim of forcing those inside to surrender.

sultan A Muslim ruler.

Thor In Norse mythology, the god of thunder and the weather.

UNESCO The United Nations Educational, Scientific, and Cultural Organization.

yurt A portable, circular tent covered with felt or animal skins, used traditionally by nomads of central Asia.

Zeus In Greek mythology, the god of the sky and thunder, and the king of the gods of Mount Olympus.

Index